Living Confidently

Living Confidently

AN 8-SESSION BIBLE STUDY ON KNOWING AND LOVING WHO YOU ARE

JOYCE MEYER

NEW YORK • NASHVILLE

Copyright © 2026 by Joyce Meyer

Cover copyright © 2026 by Hachette Book Group, Inc.

Hachette Book Group supports the right to free expression and the value of copyright. The purpose of copyright is to encourage writers and artists to produce the creative works that enrich our culture.

The scanning, uploading, and distribution of this book without permission is a theft of the author's intellectual property. If you would like permission to use material from the book (other than for review purposes), please contact permissions@hbgusa.com. Thank you for your support of the author's rights.

FaithWords
Hachette Book Group
1290 Avenue of the Americas, New York, NY 10104
faithwords.com
@FaithWords / @FaithWordsBooks

First Edition: April 2026

FaithWords is a division of Hachette Book Group, Inc. The FaithWords name and logo are registered trademarks of Hachette Book Group, Inc.

The publisher is not responsible for websites (or their content) that are not owned by the publisher.

The Hachette Speakers Bureau provides a wide range of authors for speaking events. To find out more, go to hachettespeakersbureau.com or email HachetteSpeakers@hbgusa.com.

FaithWords books may be purchased in bulk for business, educational, or promotional use. For information, please contact your local bookseller or the Hachette Book Group Special Markets Department at special.markets@hbgusa.com.

Library of Congress Cataloging-in-Publication Data has been applied for.

ISBNs: 978-1-5460-0964-1 (trade paperback), 978-1-5460-1027-2 (ebook)

Printed in the United States of America

LSC-C

Printing 1, 2026

CONTENTS

Introduction vii
Before You Start ix

Lesson 1: From Broken to Brand New 1
Lesson 2: Living Your New Life 9
Lesson 3: You Are God's First Choice 17
Lesson 4: Getting Close to God 25
Lesson 5: Everything You Need Is in Christ 31
Lesson 6: Becoming Who God Says You Are 39
Lesson 7: Standing Strong in God's Truth 47
Lesson 8: Christ at the Center 53

Looking Back 61

INTRODUCTION

Confidence is a quality that most people admire and want but sometimes struggle to develop.

The good news is that confidence is something anyone can have. No matter where you've been or who you are, you can live with confidence—real, unshakeable confidence that is rooted in Christ.

Over the years, I have learned what true confidence really is—and what it's not. Growing up, I endured abuse that shattered my confidence and distorted the way I saw myself. As I came to understand the freedom that comes from placing your confidence in Christ, my life and perspective began to change, and I want you to experience that transformation, too.

Confidence in Christ simply means trusting Him to enable you to do whatever you need to do. It's not about being fearless or having it all together. It's about knowing deep in your heart that God loves you, that you've been made right with Him through Jesus, and that He will equip you for everything He's called you to do.

I often say, "An unbeliever with confidence will accomplish more than a believer without confidence." That's how vital I believe having the right kind of confidence is. Without confidence, life is filled with self-doubt and misery. Fear and uncertainty hold you back. You miss out on new opportunities. You miss out on many wonderful things instead of stepping into the rewarding life God has prepared for you. That's why I wrote this study—to share principles that will help you live a life where your

Introduction

confidence is firmly in Christ. You'll learn to see yourself as God sees you, rest in His love, and step boldly into life with assurance that comes from Him alone. When your confidence is in Him, you can embrace new things, experience deep fulfillment, and truly love who God created you to be.

BEFORE YOU START

The Bible is more than a book about theology or a story about eternal life when we die. It also offers us the wisdom we need to live victorious, peace-filled, joyful lives on earth. Jesus says in John 10:10, "The thief comes only in order to steal and kill and destroy. I came that they may have and enjoy life, and have it in abundance [to the full, till it overflows]" (AMP). This verse isn't just about enjoying life when we go on vacation or when something delightful happens. John 10:10 is talking about the fact that God offers us the ability to find joy in ordinary, everyday life. If the only time we can enjoy ourselves is when something exciting happens, we will miss out on the abundant life Jesus died to give us. But if we learn to live according to God's Word, which requires study and obedience, we can savor each day.

Any time we spend in Scripture is good for us. But we need to do more than simply read God's Word; we need to study it deeply. We may read only one verse or passage for several days, but if we are really examining it and digging in to understand what it means for our lives, that's when it begins to transform us. The Bible teaches and empowers us in amazing ways, but we discover those truths only when we diligently study it.

This abundant life we're invited to live is only possible because of what Jesus has already done for us. He sacrificed Himself on the cross, bearing the burden and punishment for our sins. As promised, He rose from the dead on the third day and is now seated at the right hand of God. On

Pentecost, another promise was fulfilled, and our heavenly Father sent the Holy Spirit to be in us and with us at all times (Acts 2:1–33)—to teach us, help us, comfort us, and guide and lead us in all things.

Most of the New Testament letters, called the Epistles, were written to young churches and believers who needed to grow in their faith and learn to live God's way. The writers—including the apostles Paul, James, Peter, and John—were trying to help new believers become established in their relationship with God and learn how to live godly lives. That's why the Epistles contain not only valuable theological principles but also important practical advice for our everyday lives. I am excited to know that I will one day go to heaven, but I also want to enjoy the life God has given me today and every day until I get there.

I encourage you to take your time going through this study. Don't just read—pause to reflect. Stop at places that speak to you. Ask how they apply to your life and whether there are any changes you need to make to walk more fully in God's will.

I invite you to answer the questions included throughout this study—they're designed to help you recognize areas where you need to grow. In each lesson, you'll also find a short reading from one of my books, and I've included the titles in case you would like to explore the topics further.

I also want to suggest that you take the time to look up the Scripture references that appear throughout the study. Space does not permit us to print out each verse in full, but you can open your Bible to the references mentioned and read the Scripture passages for yourself. The effort you put into doing this will enhance your overall experience and help you truly absorb the truths of God's Word.

Remember that studying is different from simply reading. When we read, we take in information, but when we study, the information becomes revelation to us—it becomes part of us and transforms our lives and behavior in deeper ways than a quick reading does. When we dig deeper into Scripture, we uncover hidden treasures that not only help us live more fully for God but also continue to set us free—free to enjoy God and the life He has provided for us through Jesus.

LESSON 1

From Broken to Brand New

Let's Get Started

Have you ever been forgiven for something really significant? How did that experience of forgiveness affect you?

_____
_____
_____
_____

Key Scripture Reading

> *But God, being [so very] rich in mercy, because of His great and wonderful love with which He loved us, even when we were [spiritually] dead and separated from Him because of our sins, He made us [spiritually] alive together with Christ (for by His grace—His undeserved favor and mercy—you have been saved from God's judgment).*
>
> Ephesians 2:4–5 AMP

Dig Deeper

What feelings or images come to mind when you hear the phrases "spiritually dead" and "spiritually alive"?

LIVING CONFIDENTLY

_____
_____
_____
_____

Core Truth

When we enter into a personal relationship with God through Jesus Christ, we move from death to life, spiritually speaking. It's important for us to know what it means to be spiritually dead, so we can also know what it means to be spiritually alive. Ephesians 2:1–3 (AMP) helps us understand this:

> And you [He made alive when you] were [spiritually] dead and separated from Him because of your transgressions and sins, in which you once walked. You were following the ways of this world [influenced by this present age], in accordance with the prince of the power of the air (Satan), the spirit who is now at work in the disobedient [the unbelieving, who fight against the purposes of God]. Among these [unbelievers] we all once lived in the passions of our flesh [our behavior governed by the sinful self], indulging the desires of human nature [without the Holy Spirit] and [the impulses] of the [sinful] mind. We were, by nature, children [under the sentence] of [God's] wrath, just like the rest [of mankind].

Before we came alive in Christ, we were spiritually dead and separated from God because of sin. We walked in sin and followed the ways of the world. By doing so, we were unknowingly following the ways of Satan, the evil spirit who works against us and who fights against God's purpose and will. We walked in sin, perhaps not even aware we were sinning because we were dead to God, spiritually speaking. We had no relationship with God and were not in any way guided or led by His Spirit. If you remember your life before you accepted Jesus as your Savior, I am sure you remember that it was a miserable existence that was without peace and joy.

But God intervened, and even when we did not care about Him at all, He cared about us. Through Christ, He arranged for us to be delivered from the misery of sin and separation from Him. Jesus paid for you and me to be spiritually alive in Him, to be completely forgiven of our sin, and given a new life in Christ. Jesus did everything because of His love for the Father and for us, and now all we need to do is believe and surrender our lives to Him. The Ephesians had already believed and surrendered their lives to God through Christ, and Paul reminds them of what an amazing gift this is.

Paul uses only two short words to open Ephesians 2:4, but they are powerful words indeed. "But God" means that God interrupted the mess mankind was in, and because of His love, He provided an answer to the dilemma. The phrase "but God" is the transition from hopelessness to hope and from complete negativity to positivity. The people were dead in sin, but God intervened and raised them up and seated them in heavenly places because they were in Christ, and all of this is true today for everyone who believes.

We see the phrase "but God" used a few times in Scripture, and in each instance, we see God's delivering power (1 Samuel 23:14; Psalm 49:15; Psalm 73:26; Romans 5:8).

For example, Joseph's brothers hated him and tried to do everything they could to destroy him, *but God* was with him (Acts 7:9). If you know the story of Joseph, you know that although overwhelming odds were seemingly against him, he still succeeded and became great. This is because even though many were against him, God was for him.

God is for you, too, and because He is, you can overcome any obstacle in your path.

Joseph's brothers meant evil in their treatment of him, *but God* meant it for good so that many people would be kept alive during a great famine that came upon Egypt (Genesis 50:20). His brothers sold him into slavery, and he ended up in Egypt, the place where God had destined him to become great.

As another example, the apostle John writes that the devil comes to steal, kill, and destroy, *but Jesus* came that we might have and enjoy life (John 10:10).

No matter how much Satan seeks our harm and destruction, God always has a plan for our rescue and victory.

God not only raised us up when we were dead in sin, but He gave us the very life of Christ and He seated us in heavenly places. What does it mean to be seated in heavenly places with Christ? I don't want you to miss the power of this truth.

When Jesus had accomplished everything His Father sent Him to do, the Father raised Jesus up and seated Him at His own right hand, to wait for His enemies to become a footstool for His feet (Hebrews 10:12–13). In other words, Jesus is now at perfect rest and peace, and if we are seated with Him, then that same rest and peace is available to us. The next time you start to feel weighed down by your past, remind yourself that you are alive in Christ and trust Him to do what you cannot. You were once dead in sin, but now, alive in Christ, you can truly rest in Him, knowing He has wonderful things in store for your life.

Additional Reading

From *Habits of a Godly Woman*

Just as we have all sinned and fallen short of God's glory, we are also all justified and put into right relationship with God through the redemption Jesus Christ provided for us at the cross (Romans 3:23–24). To be justified by God means that our sins are pardoned and that, in His sight, we are made just as though we have never sinned. Once we receive God's forgiveness, we are clean. When He washes us from our sin, He holds nothing against us. Because this is true, we have no reason to wallow in guilt, condemnation, or anger toward ourselves. We honor God by accepting His forgiveness, not by continuing to make efforts to pay for our sin or punish ourselves for it. God has His own way of dealing with our sin, and that is to forgive it. We can't do anything to earn His forgiveness or to compensate for our sin, and if we try, we insult what He has done for us. God's forgiveness is a gift, and the proper response is for us to receive and be thankful for such a blessing.

It's important to understand that there is a difference between asking for God's forgiveness and receiving it. His forgiveness is a finished work. It's always available to you. All you need to do is repent and ask for it. But after you ask God to forgive you for something, take a moment to sit in His presence and meditate on what forgiveness really means and how much God loves you. Tell Him that you receive the forgiveness He has given you and that you are grateful for it. And when you are tempted to return to your guilt and shame

> over the sin for which you have received forgiveness, remember that God has taken your guilt away and that you can let it go—forever—just as God has.

Think About It

Before accepting Jesus as your Savior, how would you describe your life in the midst of spiritual death and brokenness?

_____
_____
_____

What are examples from your own life of God turning bad situations around, like he did for Joseph?

_____
_____
_____

Supporting Scripture

> *My flesh and my heart may fail, but God is the strength of my heart and my portion forever.*
>
> Psalm 73:26

Put It to Work

How can you apply the truth and confidence behind the phrase "but God" to challenges in your own life, trusting Him to bring something new out of what feels impossible? What is one specific challenge you're facing that you can entrust to God's redemptive power?

_____
_____
_____
_____

Your Personal Response

The first few verses of Ephesians 2 make it clear: We were dead in our transgressions. The Bible doesn't say we were "struggling" or "making mistakes," but rather, dead in our sins. This isn't a description of some people's condition—it describes everyone's reality before Christ stepped in.

Take time to write down some of the key "but God" moments in your life. These are times when you were headed down a difficult path but God showed up and changed everything. Be specific about how God unexpectedly worked and moved in your life.

Now consider this: If God was powerful enough to create the world, raise Jesus from the dead, and then resurrect you spiritually when you were dead in your sins, don't you think He can handle whatever doubts and difficulties you're facing today? What is dominating your thoughts today?

Write a prayer thanking God for what He's going to do, believing that He will show up in your situation. You might not know how He's going to do it, but you can be certain He has what is best for you in mind. The God who brings resurrection power won't leave you stranded!

_____
_____
_____
_____

LIVING CONFIDENTLY

LESSON 2
Living Your New Life

Let's Get Started

Do you ever get discouraged thinking you might not be good enough to be saved by God? What has made you feel that way?

_____
_____
_____
_____

Key Scripture Reading

For it is by grace [God's remarkable compassion and favor drawing you to Christ] that you have been saved [actually delivered from judgment and given eternal life] through faith. And this [salvation] is not of yourselves [not through your own effort], but it is the [undeserved, gracious] gift of God; not as a result of [your] works [nor your attempts to keep the Law], so that no one will [be able to] boast or take credit in any way [for his salvation]. For we are His workmanship [His own master work, a work of art], created in Christ Jesus [reborn from above—spiritually transformed, renewed, ready to be used] for good works, which God prepared [for us] beforehand [taking paths which He set], so that we would walk in them [living the good life which He prearranged and made ready for us].

Ephesians 2:8–10 AMP

Dig Deeper

What do you imagine when you think of a "master work" or a "work of art"? How would your daily life look different if you lived with the confidence that you are God's master work?

_____
_____
_____
_____

Core Truth

These are some of the most magnificent and hope-filled verses in God's Word. We don't have to try to work for and earn salvation, because it is a free gift of God's grace that can be received only by faith. Jesus bought our salvation, and faith in Him is the hand that reaches out to receive it.

Although these verses are so simple, many have great difficulty fully believing them and continue to try to earn salvation and right standing with God through their good works. Since that is not God's plan, it will never succeed, and the Bible tells us that anyone who tries to come to God through fulfilling the law is "cursed (condemned to destruction)" (Galatians 3:10 AMP).

There was a time when I tried to earn my way to salvation, as you may have, and I was repeatedly disappointed and extremely frustrated. The only way we can be saved is by grace through faith. There is no other way.

After believing I was saved by grace, I fell into the trap of trying to please God through good works. It is totally useless to try to buy something that is free and can never be purchased. God is pleased with us if we believe in Jesus. We cannot buy salvation or right standing with God through good works, giving to the poor, diligence in prayer and Bible study, or following any rules or laws that any person or church may suggest.

We do want to do good works, but we do them with a right purpose and motive and that is to glorify God and help people who are hurting. We should never do them to earn anything from God.

We have all sinned and fall short of the glory of God; therefore, we are all justified and made right with God through His grace (Romans 3:23–24). No one can take glory for themself or take credit for what God has done. There is a pride factor in our flesh that wants to earn, deserve, brag, boast, compare, and compete, but God will have none of it. We must humble ourselves and come to Him with nothing to offer except faith in Jesus.

Paul did not say that by grace you are *being* saved, or that you shall *be* saved, but that you *have been* saved. Salvation is an established work (something already finished), leaving no room for us to try to work for it, because God has already given it. If I give my daughter a lovely gift, it has already been paid for and there is no way she can pay for it again. We cannot pay for our salvation because Jesus has already paid, but we can and should respond in love and with a deep desire to be pleasing to Him in all our ways.

We have been recreated in Christ, born again so we may do the good works God planned for us and desires us to do. As born-again children of God, we have new desires and new goals. That may seem like a paradox, but it simply means this: Our good works can never in any way earn our salvation or forgiveness of sin, but Christianity without good works is no kind of Christianity at all.

Good works should be the result of Christianity—works that flow from a heart that wants to do them, never from the idea that they must be done to gain something from God. No amount of good works can make God indebted to us. But we can respond to His great and amazing love and gift of salvation by freely choosing to walk the path He planned for us to walk, doing the good works He prepared for us before the beginning of time.

> ### Additional Reading
>
> **From *In Pursuit of Peace***
>
> The Bible tells us that we are to live sanctified lives, yet it also says that God Himself will do the work to sanctify us. We are to simply put our trust in Him, stay close to Jesus, and allow Him to do the work through us, as these verses promise:
>
>> And may the God of peace Himself sanctify you through and through [separate you from profane things, make you pure and wholly consecrated to God]; and may your spirit and soul and body be preserved sound and complete [and found] blameless at the coming of our Lord Jesus Christ (the Messiah). Faithful is He Who is calling you [to Himself] and utterly trustworthy, and He will also do it [fulfill His call by hallowing and keeping you]. (1 Thessalonians 5:23–24 AMPC)
>
> According to John 6:28–29, the disciples once asked Jesus, "What are we to do, that we may [habitually] be working the works of God? [What are we to do to carry out what God requires?]"

> Jesus replied, "This is the work (service) that God asks of you: that you believe in the One Whom He has sent [that you cleave to, trust, rely on, and have faith in His Messenger]" (AMPC).
>
> Joy and peace are found in believing, according to Romans 15:13. Simple, childlike believing enables us to live with an ease that releases joy and peace. Hebrews 4 teaches us that those who have believed enter the rest of God.
>
> As believers, we are supposed to *believe*. Otherwise, we'd be called *achievers*. To truly believe, we must first learn how to *be* instead of *do*.
>
> Relax; all the good things that God has planned for you will come to you through Him, not through your works. As Romans 11:36 confirms, "For from Him and through Him and to Him are all things. [For all things originate with Him and come from Him; all things live through Him, and all things center in and tend to consummate and to end in Him.] To Him be glory forever! Amen (so be it)" (AMPC).

Think About It

In light of today's study, how would you describe the relationship between God's grace and good works?

_____
_____
_____
_____

What are ways that you still try to earn God's approval or prove yourself to Him, instead of freely accepting God's gift of grace?

LIVING CONFIDENTLY

_____
_____
_____
_____

Supporting Scripture

Therefore, since we have been justified through faith, we have peace with God through our Lord Jesus Christ, through whom we have gained access by faith into this grace in which we now stand. And we boast in the hope of the glory of God.

Romans 5:1–2

Put It to Work

Think of a situation in your life where you feel you've fallen short or like you've let God down. What steps can you take to bring the freedom of God's grace into that situation, responding to Him out of love instead of guilt?

_____
_____
_____
_____

Your Personal Response

Take a few minutes to be honest with yourself: Where are you still trying to earn God's approval? Perhaps it's at work, or in your relationships.

Look up Ephesians 2:8–10 in your favorite Bible translation and then copy the verses on the lines that follow. What do the sentences say about your salvation and purpose?

You are God's special creation, and He has given you a purpose that you are uniquely qualified to do. He designed you with a distinct personality, experiences, and talents so you can do that work. Make a list of gifts and strengths God has given you. Pray for opportunities to use those gifts for His glory and the good of others.

_____
_____
_____
_____
_____
_____
_____
_____

LESSON 3
You Are God's First Choice

Let's Get Started

Has feeling rejected ever impacted your sense of self-worth or belonging? What fears of rejection do you still carry with you?

_____
_____
_____
_____

Key Scripture Reading

Just as [in His love] He chose us in Christ [actually selected us for Himself as His own] before the foundation of the world, so that we would be holy [that is, consecrated, set apart for Him, purpose-driven] and blameless in His sight. In love He predestined and lovingly planned for us to be adopted to Himself as [His own] children through Jesus Christ, in accordance with the kind intention and good pleasure of His will—to the praise of His glorious grace and favor, which He so freely bestowed on us in the Beloved [His Son, Jesus Christ].

Ephesians 1:4–6 AMP

Dig Deeper

How does knowing that God chose you before the foundation of the world affect how you view rejection from other people?

_____
_____
_____
_____

Core Truth

Everybody wants to be chosen. Do you remember being a child waiting to be chosen for the dance team, the cheerleading squad, or a sports team? I do, and the fear of not being chosen, which meant being rejected, was agonizing. Perhaps you were not chosen for the team, the promotion at work, or the worship team at church, but God wants you to know that He has chosen you. Anyone who believes in Him will never be rejected. Knowing we are chosen by God gives us confidence to live life boldly and without fear.

We often hear the terms "election" and "predestination" in connection with these verses from Ephesians. This is simple to understand if we look at it properly.

God's Word teaches us that even if our mothers and fathers have rejected us, God will take us up and adopt us as His own children (Psalm 27:10). This verse has been very comforting to me because my natural parents did not love me as they should have. Their rejection left me with a wounded soul and with dysfunctional behavior, but knowing that God chose me, adopted me, and loves me unconditionally has brought healing and wholeness to me. That same healing is available to anyone who will receive it.

In addition to choosing us, God also predetermined that He would love us. Before you or I ever arrived on planet Earth, God had already decided that He loves us with a perfect and unconditional love. We do not have to earn God's love; He gives it as a free gift.

Has God chosen some people and not others? Absolutely not! His grace is available to all, but sadly, some will refuse to receive it. H. A. Ironside told this little story in his expository commentary on Ephesians:

> When asked to explain the doctrine of election a brother once said, "Well, it's this way, the Lord done voted for my salvation; the Devil done voted for my damnation; and I done voted with the Lord, and so we got the majority" (H. A. Ironside, *Ephesians: An Ironside Expository Commentary* [Kregel Publications, 1937; repr. 2007], 19).

God has already voted, and all we need to do is vote with Him. It is God's will that all people should be saved and come to know the truth (1 Timothy 2:4).

Just as all of us desire to be chosen, we also crave knowing that we are loved unconditionally. I think it is safe to say that we crave love and acceptance as a person dying of thirst would crave water. Sadly, people often look for the love they desire in all the wrong places and may even compromise their standards and moral values in order to get it. The only person from whom we can get complete, unconditional love is God. He offers it freely and abundantly at no cost to us. Our part is simply to believe His promise, receive it by faith, and learn to abide in it continually throughout our lives. This, of course, sounds like good news and as if it should be easy to do, but most people find the opposite to be true. Why?

Our experience with human beings is usually limited: Even if other people do love us, their love is often conditional, based on whether we please them. They give us love when we please them and withdraw it when we do not. We quickly learn that love has a price that must be paid on an ongoing basis, so we try hard to be what we think people want us to be to obtain the love and acceptance we desire. When people are disappointed in their quest for unconditional love, that deficit in their lives can morph into addictive behaviors aimed at relieving the pain of rejection they feel.

Through Jesus Christ, God has offered a solution to this problem. He offers us what we have been looking for. His love is everlasting, and it is so big that we could never measure how high, deep, long, or wide it is. It makes no sense to us because we know we do not deserve such a love as this, and because it doesn't seem reasonable or possible, we often miss it altogether. But I urge you to meditate on Ephesians 1:4–6 and other verses on God's love until the truth of those scriptures becomes a revelation in your heart. I can say with all certainty that nothing else in our lives will ever work properly until we receive God's love by faith. The knowledge that we are loved unconditionally needs to be the solid foundation of our lives. We simply believe it because God said it, and we stop trying to find a reason for it. God loves us because He wants to. It pleases Him to do so.

Additional Reading

From *Approval Addiction*

God tries to tell us in His Word how much He loves us, that He accepts us, and that even though He already knew every mistake we would ever make, He actually chose us for Himself:

> Even as [in His love] He chose us [actually picked us out for Himself as His own] in Christ before the foundation of the world, that we should be holy (consecrated and set apart for Him) and blameless in His sight, even above reproach, before Him in love. (Ephesians 1:4 AMPC)

Some people may read it but have a difficult time receiving it. They let their feelings steal the blessing of God's acceptance and approval. They let people's opinions determine their worth and value rather than relying on God's Word.

I encourage you to say out loud several times a day: "God loves me unconditionally, and He is pleased with me." The mind rejects such statements; after all, how could God, who is perfect, be pleased with us in our imperfections? The point is that God separates who we are from what we do. For example, my children are Meyers. They don't always act right, but they never stop being Meyers; they never stop being my children. Knowing they have a right heart goes a long way with me. They make mistakes, but as long as they admit them and their heart is right, I am always willing to work with them.

LIVING CONFIDENTLY

> God feels the same about us. As believers in Jesus Christ, we are God's children. We may not always act the way He wants us to, but we never stop being His children.

Think About It

How do your experiences of acceptance or rejection from other people positively or negatively affect your ability to feel chosen by God?

_____
_____
_____
_____

What obstacles hold you back from fully receiving the unconditional love that God has for you?

_____
_____
_____
_____

Supporting Scripture

Even if my father and mother abandon me, the Lord will hold me close.

Psalm 27:10 NLT

Put It to Work

Identify one area of your life where you seek acceptance from others or fear their rejection. Then write down three truths from today's study that can help you find rest in knowing you are chosen and accepted by God.

_____
_____
_____
_____

Your Personal Response

Think about a time when you felt deeply hurt by rejection. What strong feelings caused that memory to linger and still sting today?

Read Ephesians 1:4–6 several times. Then write the passage in your own words. Notice the difference between how God truly sees you and how past rejection made you feel. What a powerful contrast!

Know this truth: God chose you before He even created the world. This wasn't an afterthought or backup plan. You were His first choice, hand-picked by the Creator of the universe.

Create a personal declaration about who you are as God's son or daughter. Keep this declaration in a place where you'll see it often. The enemy wants you to forget your identity, but God wants you to walk confidently as His chosen child!

_____
_____
_____

LIVING CONFIDENTLY

LESSON 4

Getting Close to God

Let's Get Started

Have you ever felt distant from someone you love? How did you overcome that feeling of distance, or what helped you feel close to them again?

_____
_____
_____

Key Scripture Reading

> *But now [at this very moment] in Christ Jesus you who once were [so very] far away [from God] have been brought near by the blood of Christ. For He Himself is our peace and our bond of unity. He who made both groups—[Jews and Gentiles]—into one body and broke down the barrier, the dividing wall [of spiritual antagonism between us], by abolishing in His [own crucified] flesh the hostility caused by the Law with its commandments contained in ordinances [which He satisfied]; so that in Himself He might make the two into one new man, thereby establishing peace. And [that He] might reconcile them both [Jew and Gentile, united] in one body to God through the cross, thereby putting to death the hostility.*
>
> Ephesians 2:13–16 AMP

Dig Deeper

What does it mean for you to be "brought near" to God in Christ?

_____
_____
_____
_____

Core Truth

Our reading today says we have been brought near to God. Even though we were previously far away from Him because of our sin, now by the blood of Jesus we have been brought near. We can have a close and intimate relationship with God. We have been offered peace with God.

The Ephesian Christians were Gentiles. The Israelites (Jews) were in covenant with God, and circumcision was something that God required as an outward sign of their agreement to follow His laws (rules and regulations). They saw anyone who was outside of this covenant as being Gentiles and referred to them as "the uncircumcised." Their attitude toward uncircumcised people was not good. They felt they were better than the rest of mankind. Not only were they entrenched in their pride, but their pride also separated them from other people and caused them to reject the idea that others could be included in the covenant with God by and through their example and lovingkindness.

Once Christ fulfilled the Law and introduced the covenant of grace, there was no need for circumcision, but some of the Jews continued to tell the Gentile converts that they still needed it in order to be proper Christians.

Paul preached that we are saved totally by grace and not by works, yet some of the Jews had taken so much pride in their works for so long that they could not comprehend this new doctrine. They had erected a dividing wall between themselves and people from other nations and cultures for centuries. But Christ tore down this dividing wall by fulfilling the Law for us.

Our world today is filled with division, strife, and enmity. It exists between races of people, between nations, between religions, between Christian denominations, and between the rich and the poor, the educated and uneducated, male and female. Just think for a moment about how much turmoil the world is in constantly due to pride that causes division.

Satan loves division because he knows that it weakens us and causes us to be ineffective. God loves unity and teaches us that where unity exists, there is anointing (the power and presence of God) and blessing (Psalm 133). Jesus even told His disciples when He sent them out two by two to minister to people and prepare them before He came to them that they had to remain in peace (Luke 10:1–12). If we have no peace, then we have no power.

Jesus left us His own special peace when He ascended on high and also expressed the importance of holding on to it (John 14:27). Where strife exists, pride is always the root cause of the problem (Proverbs 13:10). Pride—especially spiritual pride—was a huge problem for the Jews, and it remains a problem for people today. But it need not be a problem if we all remember that Christ is our peace and He has torn down the dividing walls by letting us know that our worth and value is not in what we do or can ever do, but it is "in Him."

The Jews needed to realize that they could not keep the Law perfectly no matter how hard they tried and that they needed Jesus just as much as everyone else did. The Gentiles needed to realize that even though they had not been part of the Old Covenant of law and works, they were now being offered a New Covenant of salvation by grace through faith in Jesus Christ.

> ## Additional Reading
>
> **From *Do Yourself a Favor...Forgive***
>
> All the comparisons and competition in our society are very tragic and the root cause of much anger and division. Just because we are different from other people, it does not mean that we are less—or more—than they are. Everything is valuable in its own way. My hands are very different from my feet, yet they are not jealous of each other. They work together in a beautiful way, each performing the function God has designed for them. God wants us to do the same thing. He wants us to see our individual beauty and value and never feel inferior because we are different from someone else. I heard a minister put it this way: "We must learn to be comfortable in our own skin."
>
> Feelings of inferiority are often reflected through anger. We need to relate to other people as equals, with no need to feel better than them and never feeling inferior. Jesus is the great equalizer! Through Him, we are all equal. He said there is no more male nor female, Jew nor Greek, slave nor free, but we are all one in Him (Galatians 3:28). Our value is not in what we can do, but in who we are in Christ and who we belong to. We belong to God, and our looks, talents, and other abilities come from Him. A short man cannot make himself one inch taller by worrying or being jealous of someone who is taller than he is. What he can do is strive to be the best he can be in life and never compare himself to anyone else.

Think About It

What "dividing walls" exist between you and others?

_____
_____
_____

How can being brought near to God and experiencing the peace of Jesus bring new perspective to those dividing walls?

_____
_____
_____
_____

Supporting Scripture

> *By this everyone will know that you are my disciples, if you love one another.*
>
> John 13:35

Put It to Work

How has pride caused division between you and others? What steps can you take this week to begin surrendering that pride to the peace of Jesus?

_____
_____
_____
_____

Your Personal Response

We all have relationships where walls have been built between us and someone else. Sometimes those walls exist because of our own pride, and sometimes they're there because of what others have done.

But your relationship with God is different because if there's distance between you and Him, it wasn't God who built the wall. Somewhere along the way, you created that distance, whether you realized it or not.

Where do you feel the most distance from God right now? Write down those areas where you wish you felt closer to Him.

Look at Ephesians 2:13–16 and consider what the phrases "brought near by the blood of Christ" and "he himself is our peace" mean for your life today. What do they mean practically for you?

What specific steps could you take this week to experience Christ's peace in the areas where there is distance? Write down the actions you plan to take.

Finally, set aside five minutes to simply reflect on God's nearness. Thank Him for His comforting presence, and then take another five minutes to rest in it.

_____
_____
_____
_____
_____
_____
_____

LESSON 5
Everything You Need Is in Christ

Let's Get Started

Do you ever feel insufficient, like you don't have what it takes to face your challenges and circumstances? How does that feeling affect your actions or the way you live?

_____
_____
_____
_____

Key Scripture Reading

> *For God was pleased to have all his fullness dwell in him, and through him to reconcile to himself all things, whether things on earth or things in heaven, by making peace through his blood, shed on the cross. Once you were alienated from God and were enemies in your minds because of your evil behavior. But now he has reconciled you by Christ's physical body through death to present you holy in his sight, without blemish and free from accusation—if you continue in your faith, established and firm, and do not move from the hope held out in the gospel. This is the gospel that you heard and that*

has been proclaimed to every creature under heaven, and of which I, Paul, have become a servant.

Colossians 1:19–23

Dig Deeper

What does it mean to you to be reconciled to God and called "holy in his sight" through Christ?

_____
_____
_____
_____

Core Truth

Before Adam and Eve sinned in the garden (Genesis 3:6), God had a plan to reconcile everything back to Himself—a plan to restore fellowship between humanity and Himself and bring all things back into balance. The devil will not succeed in thwarting God's plan, because it has already been completed in Christ. Everyone is not living in its fullness, but it is a finished work. Until we get to heaven, no one will ever achieve perfection. But as we continue in God's Word, we are transformed "from glory to glory" as we grow and mature in Him (2 Corinthians 3:18 KJV). Even while we're here on earth, we can experience and display the fullness of everything God has for us.

To reconcile is to restore friendly relations between two parties. It means to cause people to live in harmony. It is a beautiful thought that Christ has restored friendly relations between us and Father God.

Sin separates us from God, but Christ accomplished the work of reconciling us to Him through His death on the cross. Peter writes: "For you know that it was not with perishable things such as silver or gold that you were redeemed from the empty way of life handed down to you from your ancestors, *but with the precious blood of Christ*" (1 Peter 1:18–19, emphasis mine).

God planned for our salvation and redemption from the foundation of the world. He knew that human beings would sin, but God is never without a plan and a remedy suitable to fix any problem. He planned in the fullness of time to send Jesus, His only Son, to pay for our sins. We cannot take any credit for our salvation. God planned, Jesus paid, and our part is merely to believe and receive.

Someone once asked a little boy if he had found Jesus. He answered, "I didn't know He was lost, but I was, and He found me." Again and again, believers are spoken of as the chosen of God. Let this reality sink into your soul: You are chosen! God wants you. He accepts you. He has adopted you.

When Jesus poured out His blood on the cross and suffered in agony, He did it to buy us back from the devil, who alienated us from God and wants to keep us alienated from Him. But as believers, we belong to God. We don't belong to the world or to the enemy. We are reconciled to God through Christ. We are in right relationship with Him through Christ. And we are "holy in his sight."

When Christ comes to live in a believer's heart, He plants His very life within us. Jesus is called the "Seed" (Genesis 3:15 AMP), and the "seed" of everything God is and has is inside us. As a believer, you have seeds of goodness, love, peace, joy, righteousness (right relationship with God), and more—but they don't produce a harvest overnight. In time, as you continue to walk with God and grow in your knowledge of Him, those seeds develop into good fruit in your life that pleases God and draws others to Him.

You already have everything you need in Christ. As you stay rooted in His Word and spend time with Him, you will see steady progress, little by little, and become more like Christ each day.

Additional Reading

From *Approval Addiction*

According to 2 Corinthians 5:21, we have been made the righteousness of God in Christ. The phrase "in Christ" used in verse 19 of that chapter is one that must be understood if we are to walk in victory. What we are in Christ is very different from what we are in ourselves. In and of ourselves, we are absolutely nothing of any value, but "in Christ" we partake of everything He deserved and earned. The Bible says we are "joint-heirs" with Christ (Romans 8:17 KJV). In Him, we share His inheritance, His righteousness, and His holiness.

Learn to identify with Christ; see yourself as "in Him." The Bible teaches us in Romans chapter 6 that when He died, we died, and when He was raised to a new life, we were raised with Him. If we were to place two coins in a jar, seal the jar, and submerge it in water, the coins would be in the water just as much as the jar is. Actually, though, the coins would be better off, because they would be in the same place as the jar but they wouldn't get wet.

> We may use this analogy to better understand what it means to say we are "in Christ." Jesus is the jar and we are the coins. All those who are believers in Jesus Christ are considered to be "in Him." What Jesus went through in His experience, we share. Even though we have not had the actual experience of going through it, it becomes ours through faith in Him.

Think About It

When have you experienced reconciliation personally, either with God or with someone else in your life?

_____
_____
_____
_____

How does relying on your own strength keep you from living in the completeness of Christ?

_____
_____
_____

Supporting Scripture

For in Christ all the fullness of the Deity lives in bodily form, and in Christ you have been brought to fullness.

Colossians 2:9–10

Put It to Work

Think of one or two areas of your life where you feel inadequate or incomplete. What truths from today's lesson can you apply to those areas to experience the fullness of Christ? What is one practical step for each area that you can take this week to live fully in Him?

_____

_____

_____

Your Personal Response

Far too many people walk around feeling like they're not good enough. They may feel they don't measure up in their relationships, their jobs, their parenting, or their spiritual life. This "not enough" feeling is practically everywhere you look—even among Christians.

But Scripture makes it clear and declares that you are holy in God's sight. When God looks at you, He doesn't see wrinkles, spots, or imperfections. This is not because of your performance, but because of Christ in you.

Take out your pen and list all the ways you've been reconciled to God through what Jesus did. Then write down how this amazing reality makes you feel when you really let it sink in.

Now, be honest with yourself: Where are you still trying to earn what Jesus already paid for? Identify one area where you might be wearing yourself out trying to deserve what has already been given freely.

What would your day-to-day life look like if you truly lived in the reality that you are good enough because of Jesus? If you woke up tomorrow absolutely convinced of this truth, how would your thoughts, words, actions, and relationships be different?

Remember, God isn't waiting for you to get your act together—He's waiting for you to accept what He's already done!

LESSON 6
Becoming Who God Says You Are

Let's Get Started

When did you become a believer in Christ, and what led to that decision?

_____
_____
_____
_____

Key Scripture Reading

So then, just as you received Christ Jesus as Lord, continue to live your lives in him, rooted and built up in him, strengthened in the faith as you were taught, and overflowing with thankfulness.

Colossians 2:6–7

Dig Deeper

Thinking about this verse and what you learned in the previous lesson, how would you describe what it means to live your life in Christ Jesus?

_____
_____
_____

Core Truth

Paul encourages the Colossians to continue to live in Christ in the same way that they received Him as Lord. They received Him as we do—by grace through faith (Ephesians 2:8–9)—and we also live our lives in Him continually by faith. According to Colossians 1:4, faith is leaning "on Him with absolute confidence in His power, wisdom, and goodness" (AMP).

There are two little words in Colossians 2:6 that can change your life forever: "in him," meaning *in Christ*. Paul has an amazing revelation on this subject and writes about it often. Later in this section, I will list several places he writes about this in Colossians, but he writes about it in his other epistles, too. "Who we are in Christ" is our identity as believers. We do not have to let our own thoughts and opinions or those of other people define who we are. The Word of God tells us who we are in Him. Some people have had their identity stolen by the devil because they lacked knowledge of the truth, but it is not too late to overturn all the damage the devil has done.

When you became a believer, you began your journey in Christ. When you received Him as Savior, He came to live in your heart. The way to become firmly established in your identity as a believer is to look up all the scriptures that talk about being "in Him" and mark them in your Bible, study and meditate on them, and ask the Holy Spirit to cause them to take root in your heart and mind. You can also use the "Knowing Who I Am in Christ" list on our ministry website (joycemeyer.org/InChrist) to discover more about all that is yours in Him.

When we know who we are in Christ, our confidence is not based on what people think about us, whether we are invited to certain parties or events, whether we get the job we want, whether we are welcomed into social circles, whether we get a date with the person we have a crush on, or whether anything else happens in the circumstances of our lives. It's not that we don't want acceptance or enjoy those types of things. No one wants to feel disappointed or rejected. But when we know who we are in Christ, we can get through the challenges we face while remaining confident that our worth and value do not depend on any of them going our way. Our significance is found in Christ alone.

If you learn what the Bible says about who you are in Christ and begin to study and meditate on these truths, especially confessing them aloud over and over, it will change your life. You will understand who you really are, and that will change the way you see yourself, the way you relate to other people, your perspective of your future, and other important things.

Below I list several Scripture declarations that show you who you are in Christ to give you an idea of how powerful they are. These are all from Colossians, so just imagine what you could learn if you were to study everything the Bible says about who you are in Christ. If you study and meditate on these truths, they will make an amazing difference in your life.

- I am strengthened with all power according to God's glorious might (Colossians 1:11).
- I have been rescued from the dominion and the power of darkness and brought into God's kingdom (Colossians 1:13).
- My life is rooted in my faith in Christ, and I overflow with thanksgiving for all He has done for me (Colossians 2:7).
- I am complete in Him who is the head over all rule and authority—of every angelic and earthly power (Colossians 2:10).
- I have been buried with Christ in baptism and raised with Him through faith (Colossians 2:12).

- I have been made alive with Christ, and I have been forgiven of all my sins (Colossians 2:13).
- I am renewed in the knowledge of God and no longer want to live in my old ways or nature before I accepted Christ (Colossians 3:9–10).
- I am chosen and dearly loved by God (Colossians 3:12).

Don't forget to check out the list of scriptures on our website pertaining to who you are in Christ.

Additional Reading

From *In Pursuit of Peace*

Our goal is not to be self-confident but to have confidence in who we are in Christ. We should know the value of being children of God and the position it gives us. As children of God, we can pray boldly in faith, knowing that God hears and answers our prayers. We can look forward to the inheritance that is ours by virtue of our personal relationship with Jesus. We can enjoy righteousness, peace, joy, good health, success in all we lay our hands to do, intimacy with God through Jesus, and many other wonderful benefits.

We can develop godly character and be used mightily by God to lead others to Christ and help people who are hurting. Yes, our lives can be amazingly wonderful through Jesus; however, Satan is the deceiver, and as such, he seeks continually to steal what Jesus died to provide for us.

If you are not at peace with yourself, you won't enjoy your life. You are one person you never get away from, not even for one second!

> You are everywhere you go; therefore, if you don't like and accept yourself, you cannot possibly be anything other than miserable. Also, if we don't accept ourselves, we will find it hard, if not impossible, to accept others.
>
> Our faults stand between us and self-acceptance. We think that if we could only behave better, we could like ourselves. We are proud of our strengths, natural gifts, and talents, but we despise and are embarrassed by our weaknesses. We rejoice in our successes and feel depressed about our failures. We struggle and strive for perfection, but somehow it always eludes us. Our pursuit is in vain.
>
> If God loves us unconditionally, then we can love ourselves unconditionally. And if He accepts us, we should be able to accept ourselves, too. Peace within ourselves is based on God having made us righteous in Christ.

Think About It

What changes have you noticed in yourself or in your life since you received Christ as your Savior?

_____
_____
_____

In what ways do you struggle to fully and confidently live out your identity in Christ?

_____
_____

LIVING CONFIDENTLY

_____
_____

Supporting Scripture

> *Therefore, if anyone is in Christ, the new creation has come: The old has gone, the new is here!*
>
> 2 Corinthians 5:17

Put It to Work

Think of one area of your life in which you've been defining yourself by how others see you. Write down two or three truths about your identity in Christ that replace those false identities. Take time throughout this week to meditate on these truths, remind yourself of them, and even speak them out loud, so you'll be strengthened against the lies that try to define you.

_____
_____
_____
_____

Your Personal Response

Reflect on whether you still wrestle with old labels, such as "not good enough," "failure," "damaged goods," or "unlovable." Write down the ones that have tried to define you even after you became a Christian.

Review the reminders earlier in this lesson about who you really are in Christ. Pick three powerful sentences that describe how Jesus sees you now. Turn each one into a bold "I am" statement, such as "I am chosen," "I am complete," or "I am accepted."

Once you have written them down, stand up and say them out loud! These aren't just nice affirmations—they're God's truth about you. Commit to making them part of your daily thoughts, and look for additional promises in the Bible. Remember, the devil hates when you speak your true identity out loud.

_____
_____
_____
_____
_____
_____
_____
_____

LESSON 7

Standing Strong in God's Truth

Let's Get Started

Imagine a healthy tree with deep roots. How do strong roots enable trees like this to stay secure and healthy, even through storms and wind?

_____
_____
_____

Key Scripture Reading

So then, just as you received Christ Jesus as Lord, continue to live your lives in him, rooted and built up in him, strengthened in the faith as you were taught, and overflowing with thankfulness.

Colossians 2:6–7

Dig Deeper

What does it look like to be "rooted and built up" in Christ?

_____
_____
_____

Core Truth

Looking again at Colossians 2:6–7, today I want to focus on Paul's comment in verse 7 about being "rooted and built up" in Christ. We see deep roots in the natural world, and that is how we should be in our spiritual lives. I like the way the Amplified Bible, Classic Edition renders Colossians 2:7 for several reasons. One reason is that it reads as an instruction: "Have the roots [of your being] firmly and deeply planted [in Him, fixed and founded in Him], being continually built up in Him, becoming increasingly more confirmed and established in the faith, just as you were taught, and abounding and overflowing in it with thanksgiving."

When Paul writes about "the roots of your being," he is referring to the depth of your inner life. We all have an inner life and an outward life. The outward life is what we present to other people. It may include the way we dress or style our hair, our behavior, the car we drive or the house we live in, our education, job, hobbies and interests, or our social networks and connections.

The inner life is what happens on the inside of us, where other people cannot see it. It is its own world of thoughts, feelings, ideas, beliefs, and decisions. This is where our hearts are and where we connect with God. In fact, the Bible says: "For behold, the kingdom of God is within you [in your hearts]" (Luke 17:21 AMPC). A good life is not about what happens on the outside—our circumstances, what people think of us, or how successful we seem to be by the world's standards. A good life is about what is going on inside of us. The kingdom of God is righteousness, peace, and joy in the Holy Spirit (Romans 14:17).

I have learned that people can live under the best circumstances in the world but still be miserable if they have bad attitudes. If they think negatively or have negative emotions or do not like themselves, they will still be unhappy. On the other hand, people can face all kinds of challenges in their circumstances and still be joyful.

There are people in the world today facing financial trouble, family problems, health challenges, and all kinds of struggles, yet they know and trust the Lord, and they find joy and strength in Him. With the right mindset, a happy heart, a good attitude, and the confidence that God loves you, your inner life is strong, peaceful, and joyful. You can make it through life's tests and trials, and they don't even have to seem like major obstacles. They may still pose challenges for you, but they will not be made easier by a bad attitude, wrong thinking, or negative emotions.

A second reason I appreciate the Amplified Bible, Classic Edition of this verse is that it emphasizes being rooted in Christ by saying "deeply planted." I like this because there is a difference between things that are shallowly planted and those that are deeply planted. When a storm comes, a newly planted small tree might be uprooted because its roots are too shallow. In contrast, a fully grown oak tree with a root system that reaches deep into the ground is more able to withstand storms or strong winds.

The way to stand firm in faith is to be deeply planted and to grow deep roots in Christ. Anything that is deeply rooted also gets built up and strengthened, as Colossians 2:7 indicates. When the summer has been very hot with little rain, a deeply rooted tree can still find water deep in the earth, where its roots are. Younger trees without deep roots may not survive a hot, dry summer.

No one has ever heard enough of God's Word. We need more and more of it, every day. We need to know the truth that's found within it. It always strengthens us, always helps us, and always leads us to victory.

Additional Reading

From *Habits of a Godly Woman*

To gain and maintain peace in our hearts, we must make decisions based on what God's Word says, not on what we think, what other people tell us to do, or what we hear and see in the media or on the internet.

Many people go through life making decisions on their own, without consulting the most reliable resource book ever written—the Bible—and too often their decisions bring heartache and trouble. But we can avoid negative outcomes if we seek direction and guidance in God's Word and allow the peace of Christ to rule in our hearts.

No matter what's going on in your life—and especially when you feel upset—you can look to God's Word, find a verse that calms you, and let His peace guide your decisions and settle the questions that are on your mind once and for all. Allowing the Word to dwell in your heart and mind will give you the insight, knowledge, and wisdom you need (Colossians 3:16). You won't have to wonder, "Which direction should I go?" The Word will be a lamp to your feet and a light to your path (Psalm 119:105), and choosing to honor and obey it will bring you peace.

Think About It

How have you experienced the safety of being rooted in Christ despite storms or times of difficulty?

Standing Strong in God's Truth

_____
_____
_____

What is one place in your life where your spiritual roots need to be more deeply planted in Christ?

_____
_____
_____

Supporting Scripture

They will be like a tree planted by the water that sends out its roots by the stream. It does not fear when heat comes; its leaves are always green. It has no worries in a year of drought and never fails to bear fruit.

Jeremiah 17:8

Put It to Work

Like the roots of a tree seek water, we should also seek God. Spend time with Him in His Word and in prayer and thanksgiving. When storms come in your life, let the roots of your being sink deeper into God and you will find your peace in Him. How will you spend time with God this week, other than this study?

_____
_____
_____

LIVING CONFIDENTLY

Your Personal Response

Why are tree roots so important? How does a good set of roots secure a tree during a storm? Do a little research about roots and write down what you learn. How does this relate to having strong roots in your spiritual life?

Think about a time when life hit you hard—whether long ago or recently. How did your spiritual roots help you stand strong? Looking back, how might you have benefited from deeper roots?

Where do you specifically need your roots to grow deeper right now? Is it in your prayer life, the time you spend studying the Bible, or learning to trust God when things don't make sense? Write these down as a commitment—practical ways to deepen your roots and prepare for future storms.

Remember, nobody builds deep roots overnight. It takes consistency and determination, but you can start today!

_____
_____
_____
_____
_____
_____
_____

LESSON 8

Christ at the Center

Let's Get Started

In your experience, what qualities make someone a good leader?
___
___
___
___

Key Scripture Reading

And he is the head of the body, the church; he is the beginning and the firstborn from among the dead, so that in everything he might have the supremacy.

Colossians 1:18

Dig Deeper

What does it mean to you that Christ is the head of the church?
___
___
___
___

Core Truth

The theme of Paul's letter to the Colossians is the headship of Christ. He is over and above everything. He is the head, and we are the body (Ephesians 1:22–23). He is in control, and we are to follow His instructions and example. As long as the body takes direction from the head, we will be in good shape. But when the body starts trying to be in control, that's when things become disorderly, confusing, and out of balance.

Even though Christ is the head and we look to Him to know what to do, this does not mean that believers have no responsibility or free will. God always allows us to choose whether or not we will begin to follow Him. If we do, we have certain responsibilities. Our primary responsibility is to mature spiritually and represent God by really living out the resurrection life Jesus offers us.

Paul writes about the resurrection life in Philippians 3:10, when he talks about knowing Christ and "the power of his resurrection." That means you can be right here on earth, going to work, coming home, doing the dishes, cutting the grass, and moving through everyday life and still live in the power of Jesus' resurrection. The resurrection life available to Christians does not guarantee you will never have problems; it simply offers us a place in Christ to rise above the storms of life because we know that Christ is our head and He is in control of everything.

If we do not relate to Jesus as our head—if we do not give Him first place in our lives—then whatever we do put in first place will be an idol to us. The apostle John writes, "Dear children, keep yourselves from idols" (1 John 5:21). All sorts of things try to become idols, meaning they will fight for first place in our lives. Many of these will be things that are considered "good," such as family, working hard, friends, or even serving God in ministry.

I urge you to guard against any sort of substitute that would try to supersede Him and take first place in your life. Do you know that it's possible for anything to become an idol in our lives, even the things you'd never expect? There was a time in my life, many years ago, when the ministry I was trying to build—the ministry God gave me—became more important to me than God. I did not mean for that to happen, but it did. It can happen to anyone. I was so proud of myself because I was in ministry, working for God and serving on the staff of a well-known church in St. Louis. When I looked at my life, I thought I was doing so well. But one day the Lord spoke clearly to my heart: "You are proud of yourself because you are working *for* Me. The problem is that you are not spending any time *with* Me." That was an important lesson for me to learn, and I have never forgotten it.

I want to take a moment to encourage those who work in full-time ministry: Be careful; be alert and diligent not to allow the growth or popularity of your ministry to become more important to you than God. I spend personal time with God every morning before I even think about trying to get a message to give to someone else. I focus on the things that are going on between God and me, because it is useless for me to teach a biblical message to an audience if I am ignoring God in my personal life or not listening to what He is saying to me.

Whether you serve in ministry or not, nothing is more important than your relationship with God. Keep Him first in all things, and everything else will fall into its proper place.

When we put Jesus first, we acknowledge that He is the head and we are part of the body, and we surrender everything about ourselves to Him. This idea makes some people nervous, because they are afraid that if they put Jesus first, they may have to give up something that really means a lot to them. The psalmist David writes about this in Psalm 37:4: "Take delight in the Lord, and he will give you the desires of your heart." I can personally assure you: If you put Jesus first, you will be amazed at how much God will do for you. His joy and peace will fill your heart, and you will receive the desires of your heart in God's perfect timing. This doesn't mean you won't have challenges, but you will be able to overcome them by the power of the Holy Spirit and live your life by His grace.

Additional Reading

From *Habits of a Godly Woman*

One of the greatest benefits of taking time to focus on God's presence is an inner sense of peace, joy, contentment, unconditional love, and being led by the Holy Spirit—a deep, lasting satisfaction that cannot be found in any other source. Unfortunately, there are many men and women—even Christians—who try to find fulfillment in a variety of other places. They pursue worldly things—money, promotions, positions, and relationships—hoping to find the happiness that eludes them. I did this for a number of years when I first started walking with the Lord, but when I became tired of living a powerless life, I cried out to God for help.

That's when God began to teach me that I needed to put Him first. He led me to several scriptures, including Psalm 91:1–2, which says, "He who dwells in the secret place of the Most High shall remain stable and fixed under the shadow of the Almighty [Whose power no foe can withstand]. I will say of the Lord, He is my Refuge and my Fortress, my God; on Him I lean and rely, and in Him I [confidently] trust!" (AMPC). In other words, when we spend time with God, we learn how to dwell in the secret place of His presence. And as we do, we experience an unshakable stability full of peace, power, and protection.

It is important to remember that doing things for God does not replace spending time with Him. You may serve on church committees, sing in the choir, lead a small group, or volunteer to teach vacation Bible school, but none of these activities can take the place of spending personal time with God.

Think About It

How have you experienced the joy of putting Christ first in your own daily life?

_____
_____
_____
_____

How would making Christ the center of your life change your confidence level?

_____
_____
_____
_____

Supporting Scripture

And God placed all things under his feet and appointed him to be head over everything for the church, which is his body, the fullness of him who fills everything in every way.

Ephesians 1:22–23

Put It to Work

Identify one part of your life that you can work on surrendering more fully to Christ's leadership this week. What reminders can you use throughout the week to help you stay under Christ's headship and care?

_____

_____

_____

_____

Your Personal Response

Let's get real about idols. What things tend to take first place in your life? Is it your career? Your children? Your friendships? Your desire for comfort and ease?

Take a few minutes to write down your thoughts about the areas that sometimes become idols for you. Where do you feel the need to surrender more fully to Christ's leadership? Don't rush through this exercise—this is an important step.

Next, write a prayer that acknowledges these specific areas. Then consider why it happens. Is it fear? Pride? The need for approval? Ask God to guide you and become the center of every part of your life.

Christ at the Center

Remember, putting Christ first doesn't mean you lose everything else. It means everything else finds its proper place. When He's truly first, everything in your life works so much better!

_____
_____
_____
_____
_____
_____
_____
_____

LOOKING BACK

What does it really mean to be chosen by God? How does that truth shape the way you see yourself and your worth?
_____
_____
_____
_____
_____
_____
_____
_____
_____
_____

What past experiences still cause you to feel unworthy of God's grace and love?
_____
_____
_____
_____
_____
_____
_____
_____
_____
_____

When has God shown His faithfulness by rescuing you or redirecting your steps? How can those personal "but God" moments shape how you live going forward?

_____
_____
_____
_____
_____
_____
_____
_____

Is there anything in your life that you're tempted to put ahead of Christ? What might be keeping you from fully surrendering it to God?

_____
_____
_____
_____
_____
_____
_____
_____

How deep are your roots in Christ? What practical steps can you take to grow more firmly rooted in God's truth?

_____
_____
_____
_____
_____
_____
_____

Looking Back

Where is God inviting you to step out in faith, confident in who He says you are in Christ?

NOTES

Unless otherwise stated, scripture quotations are taken from the Holy Bible, New International Version®, NIV®. Copyright © 1973, 1978, 1984, 2011 by Biblica, Inc.™ Used by permission of Zondervan. All rights reserved worldwide. www.zondervan.com The "NIV" and "New International Version" are trademarks registered in the United States Patent and Trademark Office by Biblica, Inc.™

Scripture quotations marked AMP are taken from the Amplified Bible, Copyright © 2015 by The Lockman Foundation. Used by permission. www.Lockman.org

Scripture quotations marked AMPC are taken from the Amplified Bible, Classic Edition, Copyright © 1954, 1958, 1962, 1964, 1965, 1987 by The Lockman Foundation. Used by permission. www.Lockman.org

Scripture quotations marked NLT are taken from the Holy Bible, New Living Translation, copyright © 1996, 2004, 2015 by Tyndale House Foundation. Used by permission of Tyndale House Publishers, Carol Stream, Illinois 60188. All rights reserved.

Scripture quotations marked KJV are taken from the King James Version of the Bible.

Habits of a Godly Woman, copyright © 2020 by Joyce Meyer.

Notes

In Pursuit of Peace: 21 Ways to Conquer Anxiety, Fear, and Discontentment, copyright © 2004 by Joyce Meyer.

Approval Addiction: Overcoming Your Need to Please Everyone, copyright © 2005 by Joyce Meyer.

Do Yourself a Favor...Forgive: Learn How to Take Control of Your Life Through Forgiveness, copyright © 2012 by Joyce Meyer.

Do you have a real relationship with Jesus?

God loves you! He created you to be a special, unique, one-of-a-kind individual, and He has a specific purpose and plan for your life. And through a personal relationship with your Creator—God—you can discover a way of life that will truly satisfy your soul.

No matter who you are, what you've done, or where you are in your life right now, God's love and grace are greater than your sin—your mistakes. Jesus willingly gave His life so you can receive forgiveness from God and have new life in Him. He's just waiting for you to invite Him to be your Savior and Lord.

If you are ready to commit your life to Jesus and follow Him, all you have to do is ask Him to forgive your sins and give you a fresh start in the life you are meant to live. Begin by praying this prayer...

Lord Jesus, thank You for giving Your life for me and forgiving me of my sins so I can have a personal relationship with You. I am sincerely sorry for the mistakes I've made, and I know I need You to help me live right.

Your Word says in Romans 10:9, "If you declare with your mouth, 'Jesus is Lord,' and believe in your heart that God raised him from the dead, you will be saved" (NIV). I believe You are the Son of God and confess You as my Savior and Lord. Take me just as I am, and work in my heart, making me the person You want me to be. I want to live for You, Jesus, and I am so grateful that You are giving me a fresh start in my new life with You today.

I love You, Jesus!

It's so amazing to know that God loves us so much! He wants to have a deep, intimate relationship with us that grows every day as we spend time with Him in prayer and Bible study. And we want to encourage you in your new life in Christ.

Please visit joycemeyer.org/KnowJesus to request Joyce's book *A New Way of Living*, which is our gift to you. We also have other free resources online to help you make progress in pursuing everything God has for you.

Congratulations on your fresh start in your life in Christ! We hope to hear from you soon.

ABOUT THE AUTHOR

Joyce Meyer is one of the world's leading practical Bible teachers and a *New York Times* bestselling author. Joyce's books have helped millions of people find hope and restoration through Jesus Christ. Joyce's program, *Enjoying Everyday Life*, is broadcast on television and radio and online to millions worldwide in over 110 languages.

Through Joyce Meyer Ministries, Joyce teaches internationally on a number of topics with a particular focus on how the Word of God applies to our everyday lives. Her candid communication style allows her to share openly and practically about her experiences so others can apply what she has learned to their lives.

Joyce has authored more than 150 books, which have been translated into more than 164 languages, and over 39 million of her books have been distributed worldwide. Bestsellers include *Power Thoughts*; *The Confident Woman*; *Look Great, Feel Great*; *Starting Your Day Right*; *Ending Your Day Right*; *Approval Addiction*; *How to Hear from God*; *Beauty for Ashes*; and *Battlefield of the Mind*.

Joyce's passion to help people who are hurting is foundational to the vision of Hand of Hope, the missions arm of Joyce Meyer Ministries. Each year Hand of Hope provides millions of meals for the hungry and malnourished, installs freshwater wells in poor and remote areas, provides

About the Author

critical relief after natural disasters, and offers free medical and dental care to thousands through their hospitals and clinics worldwide. Through Project GRL, women and children are rescued from human trafficking and provided safe places to receive an education, nutritious meals, and the love of God.

JOYCE MEYER MINISTRIES

U.S. & FOREIGN OFFICE ADDRESSES

Joyce Meyer Ministries
P.O. Box 655
Fenton, MO 63026
USA
(636) 349-0303

Joyce Meyer Ministries—Canada
P.O. Box 7700
Vancouver, BC V6B 4E2
Canada
(800) 868-1002

Joyce Meyer Ministries—Australia
Locked Bag 77
Mansfield Delivery Centre
Queensland 4122
Australia
(07) 3349 1200

Joyce Meyer Ministries—England
P.O. Box 1549
Windsor SL4 1GT
United Kingdom
01753 831102

Joyce Meyer Ministries—South Africa
P.O. Box 5
Cape Town 8000
South Africa
(27) 21-701-1056

Joyce Meyer Ministries—Francophonie
29 avenue Maurice Chevalier
77330 Ozoir la Ferriere
France

Joyce Meyer Ministries—Germany
Postfach 761001
22060 Hamburg
Germany
+49 (0)40 / 88 88 4 11 11

Joyce Meyer Ministries—Netherlands
Lorenzlaan 14
7002 HB Doetinchem
+31 657 555 9789

Joyce Meyer Ministries—Russia
P.O. Box 789
Moscow 101000
Russia
+7 (495) 727-14-68

OTHER BOOKS BY JOYCE MEYER

100 Inspirational Quotes
100 Ways to Simplify Your Life
21 Ways to Finding Peace and Happiness
The Answer to Anxiety
Any Minute
Approval Addiction
The Approval Fix
*Authentically, Uniquely You**
The Battle Belongs to the Lord
*Battlefield of the Mind**
Battlefield of the Mind Bible
Battlefield of the Mind for Kids
Battlefield of the Mind for Teens
Battlefield of the Mind Devotional
Battlefield of the Mind New Testament
*Be Anxious for Nothing**
Be Joyful
Beauty for Ashes
Beginning Your Day God's Way
Being the Person God Made You to Be
*Blessed in the Mess**
Change Your Words, Change Your Life
Colossians: A Biblical Study
The Confident Mom
The Confident Woman
The Confident Woman Devotional
The Courage to Change
*Do It Afraid**
Do Yourself a Favor…Forgive
Eat the Cookie…Buy the Shoes
Eight Ways to Keep the Devil under Your Feet
Ending Your Day Right
Enjoying Where You Are on the Way to Where You Are Going
Ephesians: A Biblical Study
The Everyday Life Bible
The Everyday Life Psalms and Proverbs
Filled with the Spirit
Finding God's Will for Your Life
Galatians: A Biblical Study

Good Health, Good Life
Habits of a Godly Woman
*Healing the Soul of a Woman**
Healing the Soul of a Woman Devotional
Healing the Wounds of Rejection
Hearing from God Each Morning
How to Age without Getting Old
*How to Hear from God**
How to Succeed at Being Yourself
How to Talk with God
I Dare You
*If Not for the Grace of God**
In Pursuit of Peace
In Search of Wisdom
James: A Biblical Study
The Joy of an Uncluttered Life
The Joy of Believing Prayer
The Keys to a Happy and Healthy Marriage
Knowing God Intimately
A Leader in the Making
Life in the Word
Living beyond Your Feelings
Living Courageously
Look Great, Feel Great
Love Out Loud
The Love Revolution
Loving People Who Are Hard to Love
Making Good Habits, Breaking Bad Habits
Making Marriage Work (previously published as *Help Me—I'm Married!*)
Managing Your Emotions
*Me and My Big Mouth!**
*The Mind Connection**
Mornings with God
My Time with God
Never Give Up!
Never Lose Heart
New Day, New You
Overcoming Every Problem
Overload
The Pathway to Success
The Penny
Perfect Love (previously published as *God Is Not Mad at You*)*

Philippians: A Biblical Study
The Power of Being Positive
The Power of Being Thankful
The Power of Determination
The Power of Forgiveness
The Power of Simple Prayer
Power Thoughts
Power Thoughts Devotional
Powerful Thinking
Quiet Times with God Devotional
Reduce Me to Love
The Secret Power of Speaking God's Word
The Secrets of Spiritual Power
The Secret to True Happiness
Seven Things That Steal Your Joy
Start Your New Life Today
Starting Your Day Right
Straight Talk
Teenagers Are People Too!
Trusting God Day by Day
Uniquely You
What About Me?*
The Word, the Name, the Blood
Woman to Woman
You Can Begin Again
Your Battles Belong to the Lord*

JOYCE MEYER SPANISH TITLES

Amar a la gente que es muy difícil de amar (Loving People Who Are Hard to Love)
Auténtica y única (Authentically, Uniquely You)
Belleza en lugar de cenizas (Beauty for Ashes)
Benedicion en el desorden (Blessed in the Mess)
Buena salud, buena vida (Good Health, Good Life)
Cambia tus palabras, cambia tu vida (Change Your Words, Change Your Life)
El campo de batalla de la mente (Battlefield of the Mind)
Cómo envejecer sin avejentarse (How to Age without Getting Old)
Como formar buenos habitos y romper malos habitos (Making Good Habits, Breaking Bad Habits)
La conexión de la mente (The Mind Connection)
Dios no está enojado contigo (God Is Not Mad at You)
La dosis de aprobación (The Approval Fix)

Efesios: Comentario bíblico (Ephesians: Biblical Commentary)
Empezando tu día bien (Starting Your Day Right)
Hágalo con miedo (Do It Afraid)
Hazte un favor a ti mismo... perdona (Do Yourself a Favor... Forgive)
Madre segura de sí misma (The Confident Mom)
Momentos de quietud con Dios (Quiet Times with God Devotional)
Mujer segura de sí misma (The Confident Woman)
No se afane por nada (Be Anxious for Nothing)
Pensamientos de poder (Power Thoughts)
Sanidad para el alma de una mujer (Healing the Soul of a Woman)
Sanidad para el alma de una mujer, devocionario (Healing the Soul of a Woman Devotional)
Santiago: Comentario bíblico (James: Biblical Commentary)
Sobrecarga (Overload)*
Sus batallas son del Señor (Your Battles Belong to the Lord)
Termina bien tu día (Ending Your Day Right)
Tienes que atreverte (I Dare You)
Usted puede comenzar de nuevo (You Can Begin Again)
Viva amando su vida (Living a Life You Love)
Viva valientemente (Living Courageously)
Vive por encima de tus sentimientos (Living beyond Your Feelings)
Y que hay de mi (What About Me?)

**Study Guide available for this title*

BOOKS BY DAVE MEYER

Life Lines

"Therefore, if anyone is in Christ, the new creation has come: The old has gone, the new is here!"

2 Corinthians 5:17

"But because of his great love for us, God, who is rich in mercy, made us alive with Christ even when we were dead in our transgressions."

Ephesians 2:4–5

"He who dwells in the secret place of the Most High shall remain stable and fixed under the shadow of the Almighty [Whose power no foe can withstand].

I will say of the Lord, He is my Refuge and my Fortress, my God; on Him I lean and rely, and in Him I [confidently] trust!"

Psalm 91:1–2 AMPC

"For he chose us in him before the creation of the world to be holy and blameless in his sight. In love he predestined us for adoption to sonship through Jesus Christ, in accordance with his pleasure and will—to the praise of his glorious grace, which he has freely given us in the One he loves."

Ephesians 1:4–6